ANIMALS OF THE AUSTRALIAN OUTBACK

The Outback is the vast, remote, arid interior of Australia. The Outback has no clearly defined boundaries.

The thorny dragon grows up to 20 cm in length and can live for up to 20 years. They're covered from head to tail with spines and thorns. Thorny dragons change color depending on the temperature.

The frilled-neck lizard is a reptile that belongs to the dragon family. They are carnivores, feeding on cicadas, beetles, termites, and mice. This little lizard opens up a frill around its neck to make it look big and scary.

The inland taipan
is considered the
most venomous
snake in the world.
It is estimated that
one bite possesses
enough lethality
to kill at least 100
full grown men.
Although extremely
venomous, this
snake is quite a
shy and reclusive
snake species.

The dingo is a free-ranging dog found mainly in Australia. Dingo can reach 3.5 to 4 feet in length and 22 to 33 pounds in weight. Dingoes hunt mainly at night. They can travel 37 miles per night when they are searching for food.

The redback spider is a species of venomous spider indigenous to Australia. Redbacks eat almost any small insects that are caught in their webs. The common name redback is derived from the distinctive red stripe along the dorsal aspect of its abdomen.

Camels were
imported to
Australia in the
19th century from
Arabia, India
and Afghanistan
for transport and
heavy work in the
outback. Australia
is also home to
the world's largest
herd of camels.
Camels live on
average for 40
to 50 years.

The kangaroo is a marsupial with large, powerful hind legs, large feet adapted for leaping, a long muscular tail for balance, and a small head. Kangaroos are endemic to Australia. Kangaroos usually live to around six years old in the wild.

www.ingramcontent.com/pod-product-compliance
Lightning Source LLC
Chambersburg PA
CBHW082013160726
47999CB00008B/2805